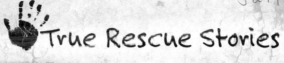

True Rescue Stories

True Wilderness Rescue Stories

Susan Jankowski

Enslow Publishers, Inc.
40 Industrial Road
Box 398
Berkeley Heights, NJ 07922
USA

http://www.enslow.com

Library of Congress Cataloging-in-Publication Data

Jankowski, Susan.
    True wilderness rescue stories / Susan Jankowski.
        p. cm. — (True rescue stories)
    Includes index.
    Summary: "Read about the 'Thirtymile Fire,' a rescue in a redwood forest, how text messaging save stranded snowmobilers, a heroic dog on Mount Hood, and a rescue on the Appalachian Trail"—Provided by publisher.
    ISBN 978-0-7660-3666-6
    1. Search and rescue operations—Juvenile literature. 2. Wilderness survival—Juvenile literature. I. Title.
    TL553.8.J36 2011
    363.34'81—dc22
                            2010005175

Printed in the United States of America

082010 Lake Book Manufacturing, Inc., Melrose Park, IL

10 9 8 7 6 5 4 3 2 1

To Our Readers: We have done our best to make sure all Internet Addresses in this book were active and appropriate when we went to press. However, the author and the publisher have no control over and assume no liability for the material available on those Internet sites or on other Web sites they may link to. Any comments or suggestions can be sent by e-mail to comments@enslow.com or to the address on the back cover.

Enslow Publishers, Inc., is committed to printing our books on recycled paper. The paper in every book contains 10% to 30% post-consumer waste (PCW). The cover board on the outside of each book contains 100% PCW. Our goal is to do our part to help young people and the environment too!

Illustration Credits: Shutterstock.com

Cover Illustration: Shutterstock.com

Contents

Wilderness Rescue Facts 4

Chapter 1
The Thirtymile Fire 6

Chapter 2
Redwood Forest Rescue 15

Chapter 3
Text Messaging Saves Snowmobilers 21

Chapter 4
Dog a Hero on Mount Hood 29

Chapter 5
**Sick Man Saved by Rescuers
in ATVs and on a Mule 36**

Words to Survive By 42
More Books You'll Like 43
Find Out More 45
Index 46

Wilderness Rescue Facts

⊠ Aluminum is an element that does not easily catch fire or burn. Its melting point is 1220.6 degrees Farenheit (660.37 degrees Celsisus). Because of its ability to withstand intense heat, aluminum is used to make airplanes and firefighting equipment.

⊠ Nurse Clara Barton founded the American Red Cross in 1881 as the nation's first disaster relief organization. Today it also helps people in trouble in small communities.

⊠ The Appalachian Trail was completed in 1937. It is a hiking trail that runs north-to-south through the mountains, forests, and pastures of the eastern United States.

⊠ Experts prevent big avalanches by setting off small bombs to cause smaller ones. Natural avalanches can move snow over 100 miles per hour. Each year, 150 people die from being buried in avalanches. (For this reason, it is very important to stay on marked hiking trails during the winter and spring seasons.)

⊠ Conifers are trees that bear cones and keep their leaves (or "needles") year round. They are known as "evergreen" trees for this reason. The fir, pine, spruce, and cedars of America's forests are all coniferous trees.

⌘ The magnetic needle on a compass always points north.

⌘ Fiberglass is the name of a product made from glass spun into a kind of yarn.

⌘ Medivac is the transport of a person to a place where he or she can get medical treatment. Medivac helicopters are often used in mountain and forest rescues. This is because it is the fastest way to transport a patient to a hospital, which may be many miles away.

⌘ In the past twenty-five years, thirty-five people have died trying to reach the summit of Mount Hood in Oregon.

⌘ The U.S. Army retired mules, donkeys, and horses from service in the middle of the twentieth century. Today, soldiers in Afghanistan are finding donkeys and mules useful in the mountains for hauling supplies and weapons.

⌘ The Federal Emergency Management Agency (FEMA) has a national certification program for search and rescue dogs and also for their handlers.

⌘ Water repellant clothing is made when the fabric is coated with rubber or plastic that is baked into the material.

Chapter 1

The Thirtymile Fire

A careless camper left a fire to smolder in Washington State's Okanogan-Wenatchee National Forest in 2001. It didn't take long for a few hot embers to turn into a thirty-mile blaze. It has gone down in history as "The Thirtymile Fire."

Rachel Welch and a crew of twenty other firefighters from the U.S. Forest Service's Naches Ranger District rushed to the scene. They began fighting the fire the way they had been trained. They dug a line around the edges of the blaze to keep it from spreading. At first, it seemed like the firefighters had the fire under control in a canyon by the Chewuch River in the northern Cascade Mountains.

An Early 'Scare'

But things had been tricky earlier that day. Squad leader Tom Craven checked around the fire line. He saw the fire was "crowning"—spreading from treetop to treetop. Tom ordered his crew to pack up its gear and cross the river to get away from the flames.

Once on the other side, everyone felt safe. The crew ate lunch. Rachel even took a short nap. Then they returned to work to pump water and dig out a fire line in other areas.

Suddenly, Tom, who was known for his smile and cheerful ways, turned very serious. Twelve years of experience helped him learn to sense when a fire was about to become dangerous.

"It's time to get out right now," ordered Tom. Then he said it again.

The huge fire was quickly spreading over the ridge of the canyon. It was coming up the road right toward the crew.

"You could see it on the road. It was just like a huge, big flame. That's all you could see was fire," Rachel later told news reporters. She and other crew members jumped into their vans and drove off to an area they thought was a safe zone.

Fire in the Sky

Once on the other side of the canyon, Rachel and the other crew members returned to work fighting the fire.

But she soon heard shouts—and orders to find shelter. Suddenly, flames were everywhere!

"It was raining embers," Welch said. "It was like the sound of a freight train. It was roaring. It was eating things up!"

Crew members scattered. Some ran for Forest Service vans; others to a sandbar; and a few others towards the road. They hurried to set up shelters. Tom and a few others ran to a field of boulders.

Rachel, just twenty-two, knew what to do. She got into her special tent-like blanket made out of aluminum and fiberglass. Once inside, she would have a better chance of surviving the flames.

Then Welch heard calls for help. Two campers, Bruce and Paula Hagemeyer, called out to her.

"Help us! Help us—we have to get into your tent!" they begged her.

Even though the tent was made for only one person, Rachel shared it with the Hagemeyers. Somehow the three of them squeezed together so they would all fit inside. Rachel became the leader of the three. She ordered Paula and Bruce to hold still and try not to rip the tent as the flames burned over them. This truly was a matter of life and death.

After what seemed like a long time, they heard

someone calling to them to get into the river. The three jumped out the tent and ran for the water.

Washington Remembers

After the biggest flames had passed, only nine of the fourteen firefighters walked out into the road. One crew member was badly burned and had to be carried out from the charred land.

Tom Craven and three of the other firefighters never returned from the wilderness. Like Rachel, they had set up their blanket shelters. But they were in the field of boulders. They perished because the air inside their shelters had become super-heated among the rocks.

By the time the fire was extinguished, even Rachel had second-degree burns on her right side. But she and the two campers had survived the raging flames. According to Deputy Forest Service Chief Jim Furnish, Paula and Bruce Hagemeyer would have likely died without Rachel's help.

Rachel was among those firefighters who became a hero on that hot, dry, July day. The fire burned 9,500 acres of the Okanogan-Wenatchee National Forest in north-central Washington. It was one of the deadliest fires in the state's history.

Smokey's Message
Not Just for Kids

Fires destroy hundreds of acres of forestland in America's West and Southwest during the summer "dry season." In the early 1940s, the U.S. Forest Service began calling upon citizens to help prevent them. People needed to learn what to do to protect forests. So the U.S. Forest Service printed posters with messages about fire safety. The first posters featured Bambi, the fawn in the famous Walt Disney movie. Then an artist drew Smokey Bear, a cartoon animal named after an outspoken New York City fire chief known for his bravery.

Ten years later, firefighters spotted a five-pound bear cub lost in the flames of a huge wildfire in Capitan, New Mexico. They rescued the cub and named it, "Smokey" after the cartoon bear on the posters. The cub's rescue drew a lot of attention across America. "Only You Can Prevent Forest Fires!" became Smokey Bear's slogan.

There are many things people can do to prevent forest fires:

◇ It is important that people make sure campfires are totally out.

◇ Grills and cook stoves must be turned off when they're not in use.

- It's always a good idea to keep a bucket of water nearby in case a cooking fire gets out of control.

- It is not safe to light matches or burn candles inside tents, which can easily catch fire.

- Smokers should never throw cigarette butts on the ground where dried leaves or twigs could smolder.

- Drivers should park their cars in cleared areas, away from trees, so no oil or gas spills in places that could ignite a fire.

- Even on holidays, fireworks are never a good idea in the forest; they can spark a flame in minutes.

- People should remember that by protecting forests, they are also protecting the animals that live there. Animals are among forest fires' first victims.

Forest Service Fall-Out

The U.S. Forest Service set up a memorial northeast of the town of Winthrop to honor the four firefighters who died trying to put out the flames. Three of them, two women and one man, were under twenty-one years-old; they had been looking forward to their futures. Squad leader Tom Craven had been the oldest. He was only thirty years old.

Their deaths greatly upset the people of Washington State. People wondered whether fire commanders could have done more to protect the firefighters at the scene. They pointed out that many of the crew members were "rookies." This means crew members were young and new to firefighting. People demanded the Forest Service investigate what went wrong during the fire to cause their deaths.

Years of arguments followed among firefighters, government lawmakers, and citizens in a United States court of justice. Some accused the crew's commander of failing to do his job. He was also charged with not being truthful about what happened when investigators asked him questions about the fire.

Yet others said it was unfair to blame the deaths on

any one person. After all, the raging fire was dangerous for everybody, including the fire commander.

Will Craven, Tom's brother, spoke up for the commander: "He's not in charge of the fire, or the wind, and that's what killed them," said Will. He also said that being a firefighter was like being a soldier at war. It's dangerous work in which the life of the firefigher is often at risk.

Firefighter Karen Fitzpatrick was only eighteen when she died in the blaze. In court, her mother wore the same wristwatch her daughter had worn while fighting the flames. The clock face stopped at 5:29 P.M., which is likely the time of Fitzpatrick's death. Her mother was among those people who were angry with the commander.

In the end, the commander said although he had not been truthful about all that had happened during the fire, he was not to blame for the deaths of the four crew members. The judge agreed.

Still, people on both sides want to know firefighters will have more protection the next time they fight a forest fire. After the tragic deaths of the crew in the Thirtymile Fire, the U.S. Forest Service reviewed its safety guidelines. It is working to improve firefighters' safety in the forest.

Each summer, wildfires destroy thousands of acres of forest during the dry summer season in America's western states. Few realize the impact of such an inferno. In the prologue to the U.S. Forest Service's investigation report the author writes, "The stillness of this place is eerie amidst the lingering smoke. The Chewuch River makes no sound as it glides by. Yet, there was violence here unimaginable to anyone who didn't witness the conflagration. Four people died here."

Chapter 2

Redwood Forest Rescue

R oy Webster and his crew were cutting down giant redwood trees on a steep hillside in northern California. After many years on the job, redwood loggers like Roy know where to stand beneath the tall trees as they saw through them. A person who is standing in the wrong place risks getting crushed when the tree falls to the ground. However, no matter how careful a logger is, there is always a risk of injury when "felling" trees. This is what many think of as "chopping them down."

Everything seemed to be going as planned for the logging crew on this autumn day. The sun shone high overhead. The loggers knew it would soon be time for them to take their lunch break. Then suddenly Roy went down! Somehow, he had fallen down the hill's slope. Worse yet, he had broken both of his legs during the fall!

Roy's crew members had to act fast. After all, Roy could do little to help himself. He was in pain and in danger of going into shock.

Dropping into a "Sea" of Trees

At noon, staff at the U.S. Coast Guard Air Station in Humboldt Bay received a call for help from somewhere in the Redwood Forest. Roy's coworker had been able to call the Coast Guard station from his cell phone. The station's commanders, a flight mechanic and rescue swimmer, hurried to the Coast Guard helicopter. The men were airborne within minutes after receiving the call.

After flying over a stretch of beach, the crew reached the edge of the massive forest. They caught only a quick look at the Pacific Ocean shimmering before them in the midday light. Down below, beachgoers and surfers pointed at the aircraft. Curious people watched as the helicopter headed straight for the trees.

Once over the redwoods, the crew searched for signs of loggers. It seemed like the tall redwoods went on forever. It would be easy for a hiker—or logger—to get lost in what looked like a "sea" of trees from above. Then the Coast Guard crew spotted orange flags. The loggers were waving them at the helicopter to signal to the rescuers that they were close to Roy's location. This was the break the Coast Guard rescuers were looking for!

The helicopter hovered at 100 feet above ground. With the help of the crew, rescuers were able to find Roy lying on the side of a hill. He was injured; yet he had survived the fall.

Rescuer Chuck Brannan let helicopter crew members slowly lower him down into the canopy made by the tall redwoods. This would be his best chance to reach Roy. This was different than his usual mission. Chuck was a U.S. Coast Guard Rescue Swimmer; his job was to save people from the waters of the Pacific Ocean. He was trained to be lowered into the ocean's waves. But once his feet hit the ground, Chuck got right to work. He was able to move Roy to a stretcher with a strong harness attached to it. Then the crew above carefully hoisted the grateful Roy up into the helicopter.

Back at the air station, an ambulance stood at the ready. Medics prepared to move Roy to a nearby hospital.

In the days following Roy's rescue, local loggers wondered what had gone wrong. Had Roy been in an

The Dangers of Logging

Loggers must be strong and in good shape to do their jobs. They have to lift heavy branches and logs and climb up tall trees. Sometimes they work in bad weather; if conditions are bad enough, loggers may have to stop work for the day. It simply becomes too dangerous. High winds and heavy rain can make climbing tricky. A person can easily slip. Also, it is harder to use a chainsaw under these conditions.

It takes practice to learn how to safely use a chainsaw. It is also a special skill to learn where to cut a tree and then where to stand before it falls. Falling branches are also a threat; a logger could be injured should a branch fall on his or her head. For this reason, many loggers wear helmets for protection.

Hidden rocks or mud can cause problems for the vehicles loggers use to lift and haul trees. Rocks can get caught in the engine and shut the vehicle down. Or, a rock can fly out from beneath the vehicle like a bullet and injure a logger. Many wear goggles to protect their eyes. They also wear thick boots to protect their feet. Some of the motors that run logging machinery are very loud. Loggers sometimes wear earplugs or ear coverings to protect their hearing.

Working outdoors in extreme heat or cold for long periods of time can be risky. A person can suffer from a heat stroke in the summer or frostbite in winter. Whenever a person plans an outing in the forest, it is important to wear the right clothing, bring the right safety gear, and carry a cell phone.

unsafe position? Or, had he come upon loose ground? No matter the cause, Coast Guard rescuers were there to pull him from the shadows of the huge redwoods. The logging crew had done their part as well. They brought a fully charged cell phone, as well as orange emergency flags, to the site. Paying close attention to details like these make a difference when working in the wilderness.

Timber!

The Redwood Forest spans the northern part of California and the southern part of Oregon. There are 200 miles of hiking trails winding through it. Parts of these trails border the 37 miles of nearby Pacific Ocean coastline next to the forest. There are a number of small timber towns along the Pacific Coast. But today, in towns like Orick, many people work in shops, motels, and restaurants that serve tourists instead of harvesting trees. The town is among the few places where visitors can enjoy both the amazing redwood trees and pristine ocean beaches.

There is less demand for redwood lumber than there was fifty years ago. In fact, the California Redwood Company closed its Orick sawmill in October 2009. Yet some of the local people continue to work in the timber industry. People who "fell" trees for a living have skills passed on to them by their parents and grandparents. They know the safest ways to harvest redwoods. So it was somewhat of a surprise when a logger needed the United States Coast Guard to rescue him in the Redwood Forest.

Chapter 3

Text Messaging Saves Snowmobilers

If a person gets lost in the forest, the first step for survival is to call for help. In the past, this meant the person in trouble had to find dry wood and start a small, smoky fire. Rescuers might then see the smoke from that fire rising above the trees. But at times this may be difficult. There is always the risk of that fire burning out of control. Or, the person may be injured and unable to gather wood. If conditions are wet, it may be hard to get anything to burn. Today, cell phones are a better and much faster way to call for assistance.

John Rocky and his son, Tim, were no strangers to snow. They're from Cold Springs, Minnesota, where it snows throughout that state's long, cold winters. The father and his adult son looked forward to a visit to the Arapaho National Forest in Rocky Mountain National

Park, Colorado, during the last few days of 2008. They had planned the trip as a holiday vacation.

Snowmobile Capital of Colorado!

There is a snowmobile trail in the park that stretches from Grand Lake for 100 miles to the start of another forest. Some forest rangers call the area around this trail, "The Snowmobile Capital of Colorado," because it is so popular.

The Rocky's started their snowmobile engines in the crisp, mountain air the day before New Year's Eve. The start of their ride was fun! It felt good to be outdoors among the pine trees beneath the huge, glistening mountains. It's easy to picture father and son zipping around the trees and over the white, sparkling slopes.

Then all of a sudden, everything looked strange to both Tim and John Rocky. They soon knew they were lost. It was hard to remember which direction they had come from. Without meaning to, the Rocky's had strayed from the trail inside the park. They did not know they were outside the park in an area that is not safe for snowmobiles. It is called the Never Summer Wilderness Area.

Although it is in the Arapaho Forest, this area is

closed to snowmobilers. The snow is too deep and it is simply too dangerous to ride there. Arapaho American Indians gave this place the name, "Never Summer." This is because the deep snow often stays frozen all year in this spot.

Dangers at Night

Things got worse when father and son got their snowmobiles stuck in the deep snow of a drainage gulch. Luckily, neither was hurt. But winter daylight time was short and it would soon be dark. The men knew they had to survive the night in the forest. They were over ten thousand feet above sea level. As the sun set, temperatures dropped to below 10 degrees Fahrenheit; this is well below freezing. The two men were able to build a fire—to keep warm—and also to keep the wild animals like bears and cougars away.

Just a few days before, two local snowmobilers were killed in an avalanche that happened nearby. Rangers had been unable to dig them out from under the snow in time to save their lives. Avalanches are always a danger in the mountains. This is especially true in the spring as snow begins to melt. Yet an avalanche can happen any time of year if weather conditions are right. Engineers do what they can to protect national park areas from avalanche danger. They close certain parts of the parks in winter when they cannot.

John and Tim knew that if they were to survive, they would have to remain calm and call for help. They had come prepared. Both John, forty-nine, and Tim, twenty, had worn the right clothing. They also carried a fully charged cell phone.

Meanwhile, rangers received a report telling them two men were missing. They sent out search and rescue teams (SAR), who scanned the forest from midnight until four o'clock in the morning with no luck. Then they took a break and waited for the sun to come up.

After the sun rose the next morning, John and Tim Rocky got busy with the business of survival. At about nine o'clock, they sent text messages to their family that probably read something like the code words below:

STUK N SNO
STARTD FIRE2KEEP WARM
LOST
HELP

Hi-Tech Response

Not only was text messaging a good way for the men to let their family know they were in trouble, but it also helped rangers locate them. John and Tim had survived the cold night! A family member was thrilled to learn the two men were still alive and forwarded the text message to the ranger station. Time seemed to pass quickly as District Ranger Mark McCutcheon and two other forest rangers traced the electronic signal from the men's cell phone. They used the trace to make a map and directions to their location.

Rescuers skied three miles to get to the area where they had picked up the signal. Soon they heard shouts.

"Hey, hey, hey!"

Suddenly, two men wearing red and black snowsuits pushed their way out of the trees and into the view of rescue rangers.

What a relief it must have been when Tim and John heard the voices of the rescuers! They had been hiking in three feet of snow. They were hungry, thirsty, and very, very tired.

Worse yet, they were sweating from all of the exercise of pushing through the deep snow. This meant

Snowmobile Safety

Riding snowmobiles is a favorite winter activity for many people who live in America's northern and mountain states. Wisconsin is among those states that provide safety tips for people who enjoy snowmobiles. Some of the state's safety tips are easy to follow. For example, it is important to travel at a speed that still gives the driver enough time to react if something unexpected happens. (In other words, slow down!) Drivers should go slower at sunset, when it gets harder to spot rocks, sticks, or animals on the trail.

Tips

◊ Snowmobilers should always stay on marked trails.

◊ Along the highway, drivers should stay on the right side of the road.

◊ When it is unclear whether the ice covering a pond or lake is thick enough to hold a snowmobile, it is best to avoid driving over it.

◊ It is important to wear the right gear and clothing. This includes a helmet with goggles or face shield to keep twigs and stones from hitting the eyes or face. Loose pant legs or sleeves can get caught in the engine.

◊ It is best to wear tight-fitting clothing. Coats

and leg coverings should be made of a material that repels water. It is easier to stay warm when you are dry.

◇ Always ride with a partner; never snowmobile alone.

◇ It is a good idea for both people to carry cell phones to call for help. If one of the phone's batteries gets low, there is a second phone to use to call for help.

◇ Finally, every snowmobile must have a first-aid kit on it. Besides bandages, it should contain a flashlight, knife, waterproof matches, and a compass.

they were wet. Staying dry in cold temperatures is crucial; it keeps the person from getting chilled.

The rangers gave the pair water and applesauce, which has a lot of sugar in it for quick energy. It is also easy to carry in a backpack. Then they helped John and Tim put on snowshoes. A person wearing snowshoes can walk on top of snowdrifts without sinking. This is because snowshoes spread out the person's weight to keep him or her from sinking.

Then rescuers helped the men hike back to the forest ranger station.

"They zigged when they should have zagged!" Ranger McCutcheon told reporters about the men getting lost.

"Still, they did the right things to survive," he said. The men had been missing for fifteen hours.

The father-and-son team was fortunate. They were warm and dry, and safe for the New Year.

Chapter 4

Dog a Hero on Mount Hood

Its been said that a dog is a "man's best friend." This proved to be true when three friends set out to climb to the summit of Mount Hood in Oregon. They had no idea they would be turning around. They had no idea a German shepherd named Velvet would help save their lives.

Two of the climbers were school teachers. Matty Bryant and Kate Hanlon were teachers in schools in the suburbs of Portland, Oregon. Bryant, Hanlon, and six others began the hike to climb Mount Hood on a Saturday morning. They were all experienced rock climbers. They had brought the right gear to camp overnight on the 11,239 foot (3,425.6 meter)-high mountain, which towers over the Mount Hood National Forest. They also brought a transmitter with them. This is a small device that sends and/or receives signals. If the climbers ran into trouble, rangers might be able to track their location with the transmitter.

The Weather Factor

On Sunday, the weather took a turn for the worse. Now the climbers faced strong winds and blowing snow. So tthey chose to play it safe; they turned around to go back down the mountain. They decided it was not worth risking their lives to climb to the summit of Mount Hood.

The storm picked up strength. Matty and Kate roped themselves together with another friend, Christina Ridl. They also fastened the rope to Velvet. This is so they could all stay together in the high winds and blowing snow. Plus if anyone slipped, they would still be connected to others who still had their feet on solid ground.

At about 8,300 feet (2,529.8 meters) above sea level, Matty, Kate, and Christina reached a slippery edge. First one climber, then another, then the other fell at nearly the same time! The three climbers and Velvet tumbled down nearly five hundred feet. This is like jumping off the roof of a forty- to fifty-story apartment building.

When the climbers finally hit the ground, they

knew they were lucky to be alive. Velvet, too, had survived the fall. But Ridl had injured her head. She put on a tight-fitting hat to stop the bleeding.

Meanwhile, the other climbers were doing their best to make it safely down the side of Mount Hood in the storm. Trevor Liston from Portland was one of them. He saw the three people fall who had been roped together. He and the others tried to throw a rope down to them. But this was not successful. Trevor and the other climbers called park rangers for help.

The three fallen climbers were wet and cold. But they had to keep moving to stay warm. They hiked for miles to try to make it down the mountainside. Soon it became dark. They had to face the fact they would be spending the night outdoors on the mountain—this time in bad weather.

The three did their best to stay calm. They wrapped themselves in sleeping bags to stay warm. They knew it might take some time for rescuers to find them in the dense forest. The Mount Hood National Forest spans over one million acres! The three also huddled around Velvet, who kept them warm with her fur and body heat. Velvet also helped the climbers keep their spirits up. This is important when lost in the wilderness. A person must make up his or her mind to survive.

Dogs can also be helpful because they can smell the scent of another animal. A dog may start barking to let people know danger is near. Dogs can also hear sounds that people might not hear. But perhaps their most important role is to keep people warm and comfort them. It is likely petting Velvet's black fur comforted Matty, Kate, and Christina. The same was probably true whenever the friendly dog licked their chins!

Even though they could not yet reach the stranded climbers, rescuers did their part to help them keep calm. They were able to call the climbers on their cell phones to guide them.

The three spent the night in blinding snow and 70 mile-per-hour winds. The forest was dense and dark. Snowflakes swirled around and around. The wind howled all night long; at times, it sounded like the cries of wolves! It was a long night for everyone, including Velvet. During the cold night, she stretched across the three climbers like a warm blanket.

No Place Like Home!

As soon as the sun rose over the glaciers, Erik Brom and other members of the Portland Mountain Rescue Team began their search. The rescue team found the climbers with Velvet in White River Canyon at about 7,400 feet.

"We're soaking wet and freezing!," the three told reporters who shouted questions at them. Upon her return, Christina got into an ambulance to go to the hospital. She had black rings on the skin around her eyes from her injury. Still she was willing to have her picture taken by news reporters. Everybody, Velvet included, was happy to be back at the forest ranger station in the park.

Rescuers said Velvet probably saved the climbers' lives by huddling with them during the cold night.

Russel Gubele was one of the rescue operations leaders. He warned reporters that just knowing how to rock climb does not always mean that person is ready to climb a mountain that rises out of a deep forest. Still, Matty, Kate, and Christina had been prepared with the right gear, cell phones, the transmitter, and Velvet. They had helped ensure their own rescue by being prepared.

Even though she is just a pet, Velvet turned out to be one of the operation's rescue heroes. But in the end, Velvet was probably just happy to go home.

"She'll be getting extra treats when we get home," Matty joked.

Search and Rescue Dogs

Dogs can see things humans can't see, hear things people cannot hear, and go where we cannot. Their sense of smell is much sharper than that of humans. For these reasons, dogs are ideal for search and rescue operations.

In the forests and mountains of Europe, people have used dogs in rescue operations for centuries. Sometimes they were sent ahead of rescue teams carrying water and other survival supplies. There are several breeds that seem well suited for search and rescue. Today, German shepherds are among the breeds favored by search and rescue teams. But trainers point out that good rescue dogs are not limited to one breed.

The dogs that are chosen for search and rescue duty are smart and easy to train. They also like to run and play and have plenty of energy. They must be good at picking up scents outdoors. Most important, they must like to be around people.

Trained rescue dogs find injured people after an earthquake, hurricane, or other disaster. Rescue dogs helped firefighters find people in the rubble after the September 11, 2001, attacks on the World Trade Center in New York City. They also search out missing people in the mountains or dense forests.

Earlier that year, three men who did not have transmitters, or a dog, went missing while trying to climb Mount Hood. Rangers believe they died from being outside for a long time in cold temperatures. In the past twenty-five years, thirty-five climbers have died trying to reach the summit of Mount Hood.

Chapter 5

Sick Man Saved by Rescuers in ATVs and on a Mule

T he Appalachian Trail winds over two thousand miles, spanning fourteen eastern states. It stretches from Georgia all the way up to Maine. A portion of it winds through Cherokee National Park, along the border of Tennessee and North Carolina. This is a place of amazing scenic beauty. Ross John Sieja, sixty-two, traveled all the way from Oregon in the spring of 2008 to hike part of the famous trail. He chose a part of the forest called Hurricane Gap in the eastern part of Tennessee for his journey.

Ross John had planned to hike the trail for a few days. But along the way, he began to feel weak. Soon he knew he was becoming ill. He tried his best to continue hiking. But after awhile, he knew he had to rest. He simply could not go on to complete his journey.

Mountain Shelter

Ross John found the Spring Mountain Shelter just off the trail. The shelter is located in the forest on the border of Tennessee and North Carolina. With three sides, a picnic table, and a place to lie down, the shelter seemed to be a good place to stop.

Ross John knew he needed to rest. He thought the best plan of action was to stay at the shelter and wait to be rescued. It must have been a lonely feeling to be sick in the forest without anyone there to help.

Because he was sick, he was losing track of time. He was finding it hard to remember just how long he had been at the shelter. He looked up through the fir trees and mist. Small, white flowers dotted the forest area around him. Many of these blooms would yield berries later in the season. He listened to the cheerful chirping of songbirds as clouds sailed across the sky. Now and then a turkey vulture circled above the foothills. Ross John Sieja hoped someone would find him soon.

Early the next morning, Ross John heard a sound. Voices! Some hikers had found him! The hikers saw him and ran over. One of them quickly dialed "911" to call for help from a cell phone.

A Team Effort

Greeneville (Tennessee) Emergency and Rescue Squad Captain Jon Waddell answered the call for help at 8:15 A.M. He called in emergency response units from Tennessee. A team from North Carolina came to help with the rescue, as well. Police, firefighters, search and rescue, and emergency response crews all came together to work out a rescue plan. Even staff from the American Red Cross came to give support.

Rescue teams set up a command post near a campground by Paint Creek. A team of about a dozen men drove four all-terrain vehicles (ATVs), along with two trailers, towards Hurricane Gap Road. This is the road that would lead them to the Spring Mountain Shelter and Ross John. Two rescuers went ahead of the crews to see if they could help him at the shelter. They carried medicine and other supplies.

Captain Waddell and the other rescuers worried that getting to Ross John might be a challenge. The terrain was rough and steep—maybe even too tough for hikers or ATVs. Plus, if Ross John's condition got any worse, they might have to carry him out of the forest to get him to a hospital. He was a large man and this was something rescuers needed to plan for.

Roy Darnell, who lived in nearby White Sands, and his mule, became important parts of the rescue "backup plan." Roy agreed to ride his mule on the steep trail to try to save Ross John. Roy was a relative of one of the members of the rescue team. He believed in its mission. Many search and rescue crew members volunteer. They undergo training and then help with search efforts by choice. It is not their job. This means they do not accept payment for their search and rescue services. They are willing to do it simply to help out people in trouble. Roy was one of these people.

"If ATVs could not have gotten in, we were going to try to put him on the mule," rescuer Kevin Ayers later told reporters about the plan. "He was a good, calm mule."

Kevin said Roy and his mule often volunteer their services during local rescues. He said Roy's mule is local rescuers' "backup plan."

But the crew driving ATVs reached Ross John in early afternoon. They were able to help him into one of the vehicles and drive him to safety.

Good News!

As the day wore on, word of Ross John's rescue spread throughout Tennessee's eastern towns. People talked

Search and Rescue Vehicles

When there's someone in trouble, search and rescue teams will do everything possible to get there. The vehicles they use depend on the terrain. In dense forests, rescuers will search from the ground and, if needed, from the air. Helicopters can lift rescuers high above the trees to get a bird's-eye view of the forest below. This can help them spot people in trouble.

ATVs are important rescue tools. ATVs can go where most other vehicles cannot. They can roll over rocky trails, tree roots, and different kinds of soil. They can often drive through mud. Today there are ATVs that have narrow frames, enabling them to move through tight spots and trails. Some are built with platforms that can be used as stretchers.

Sometimes rescuers need to set up a command post. Special vans and/or trailers are equipped with maps, radios, tracking devices, and a communications system. Rescue team members can talk to each other using these systems to find someone. They can contact local police and fire departments. They may want the news media to know about a missing person to urge citizens to call the police with any clues.

In deep snow, rescuers may use snowmobiles. Or they may use snowshoes to hike in on foot. Skiing is faster than hiking, but it also requires clear paths with a heavy snowpack.

There are several kinds of trucks and trailers used to help rescuers during a fire. Some carry water and hoses. Newer vehicles may carry foam sprays. At most command posts, an ambulance is at the ready to carry patients to the hospital.

In the end, a hiker must do all he or she can to be safe in the forest. Being prepared for the worst in the wilderness is the key to survival.

about it at a local festival. It was clear that search and rescue teams were ready to do "whatever it takes" to save Ross John. If the ATV's could not get to him, he would have been able to ride out on Roy's mule. Without the rescue teams, and the hikers who had called for help, Ross John Sieja might not have survived getting sick while hiking alone in the wilderness.

Words to Survive By

access—To gain entry to a place or thing.

airborne—Off the ground and in the air.

alert (alerted)—Quick in thought and action; ready.

avalanche—A mass of loose earth, rocks, or snow swiftly sliding down a hillside.

boulder—A huge rock.

canopy—A roof-like covering usually made of canvas.

condition—A state that must exist before something else can happen.

drainage—System for carrying off wastewater.

ember—Glowing piece of wood or coal from a fire.

fell—To cut down a tree.

foothill—A low hill at the base (or "foot") of a mountain.

glistening—Shining or glittering.

gulch—A deep valley cut into the earth by a stream.

harness—A strap used to fasten one thing to another.

hoist (hoisted)—To lift or pull up.

hover (hovered)—To stay in the air in one place.

ignite—Set fire to.

local—Of or from a certain place.

lumber—Wood timber sawed into boards or planks to be used as building material.

lumberjack—A old fashioned term for someone who harvests trees.

massive—Very large; huge.

pristine—Left in its natural state; untouched by people; unspoiled.

reduce—Make smaller or lessen.

repel—To drive or force back.

shelter—Something that covers or protects.

slogan—A phrase used to give a message or advertise a product.

smolder—To burn or smoke without a flame.

stretcher—A light, covered frame used to carry the sick or injured.

terrain—Landscape.

timber—Wood for building; or trees in forests.

yield—Give, pay, or produce.

More Books You'll Like

Bishop, Amanda, and Vanessa Walker. *Avalanche and Landslide Alert!* St. Catharines, Ont., Canada: Crabtree, 2005.

Costain, Meredith. *Devouring Flames: The Story of Forest Fires.* Washington, D.C.: National Geographic Society, 2006.

Kyi, Tanya Lloyd. *Rescues!: Ten Dramatic Stories of Life-Saving Heroics.* Toronto: Annick Presss, 2006.

Markle, Sandra. *Rescues!* Minneapolis, Minn.: Millbrook Press, 2006.

Find Out More

American Safety and Health Institute
<http://www.ashinstitute.org/>

Coast Guard Rescues Logger From Redwood Forest
<http://www.youtube.com/watch?v=ESRHfsgObc0>

"Dog Helps Save Stranded Mount Hood Climbers"
<http://www.foxnews.com/story10,2933,252852,00.html>

"Minnesota Snowmobilers Rescued in Colorado"
<http://www.kare11.com/news/news_article.
    aspx?storyid=534332&catid=2>

National Association for Search & Rescue
<http://www.nasar.org/nasar/>

"Oregon Hiker Rescued From Appalachian Trail"
<http://greenevillesun.com/story/294759>

Thirtymile Fire Memorial
<http://www.fs.fed.us/r6/wcatchee/fire/thirtymile/>

Index

A

Afghanistan, 5
all-terrain vehicles (ATVs), 36, 38-40
aluminum, 4, 8
American Red Cross, 4, 38
Appalachian Trail, 4, 36
Arapaho American Indians, 23
Arapaho National Forest, 21-22
avalanche, 4, 23-24
Ayers, Kevin, 39

B

Bambi, 10
Barton, Clara, 4
Brannan, Chuck, 17
Brom, Erik, 32
Bryant, Matty, 29-33

C

California, 15, 19
California Redwood Company, 19
Capitan, New Mexico, 10
Cascade Mountains, 6
cell phones, 16, 18, 19, 21, 24-25, 27, 32, 33, 37
Cherokee National Park, 36
Chewuch River, 6, 14
Cold Springs, Minnesota, 21
Colorado, 22
conifers, 4-5
Craven, Tom, 6-7, 9, 12
Craven, Will, 12-13

D

Darnell, Roy, 38-39
dog rescues, 5, 29-35

E

Europe, 34

F

Federal Emergency Management Agency (FEMA), 5
fiberglass, 5, 8
Fitzpatrick, Karen, 13
Furnish, Jim, 9

G

Georgia, 36
Grand Lake, Colorado, 22
Greeneville (Tennessee) Emergency Rescue Squad, 37
Gubele, Russel, 33

H

Hagemeyer, Bruce, 8-9
Hagemeyer, Paula, 8-9
Hanlon, Kate, 29-32
helicopters, 5, 16-17, 40
hiking, 4, 19, 25, 36, 40, 41
Humboldt Bay, 16
Hurricane Gap, 36
Hurricane Gap Road, 38

L

Liston, Trevor, 31
logging, 15-20

M

Maine, 36
McCutcheon, Mark, 25, 28
Medivac, 5
Mount Hood, 5, 29-31, 35
Mount Hood National Forest, 29, 31
mules, 5, 38-39, 41

N

Never Summer Wilderness Area,
    22-23
New York City, 10, 34
North Carolina, 36, 38

O

Okanogan-Wenatchee National
    Forest, 6, 9
Oregon, 5, 19, 29, 36
Orick, California, 19

P

Pacific Ocean, 16-17, 19
Paint Creek, 38
Portland, Oregon, 29, 31
Portland Mountain Rescue Team, 32

R

rangers, 22-25, 28, 30-31, 33, 35
Redwood Forest, 15-17, 19-20
Ridl, Christina, 30-33
Rocky, John, 21-22, 24-25, 28
Rocky, Tim, 21-22, 24-25, 28
Rocky Mountain National Park,
    21-22

S

safety gear, 18, 26-27, 29
search and rescue teams, 24, 40, 41
search and rescue vehicles, 40
September 11, 34
Sieja, Ross John, 36-38, 41
Smokey the Bear, 10

snowmobiles, 21-23, 26-27, 40
snowmobile safety, 26-27
snowshoes, 28
Spring Mountain Shelter, 37-38

T

Tennessee, 36-38
text messaging, 21, 24-25
Thirtymile Fire, 6-9, 12-14
transmitter, 29-30, 33, 35

U

U.S. Army, 5
U.S. Coast Guard, 16-17, 19-20
U.S. Forest Service, 6, 9, 10, 12-13

V

Velvet, 29-33

W

Waddell, Jon, 37-38
Walt Disney, 10
Washington State, 6, 9, 12
water repellant, 5
Webster, Roy, 15-17
Welch, Rachel, 6-9
White River Canyon, 33
White Sands, 38
Winthrop, Washington, 12
Wisconsin, 26
World Trade Center, 34

Read Each Title in True Rescue Stories

TRUE MOUNTAIN RESCUE STORIES

Shocking and triumphant true accounts of railroad wrec plane and helicopter crashes, and mountaineers who nea met their maker are featured in this collection.

ISBN: 978-0-7660-3572-7

TRUE OCEAN RESCUE STORIES

A naval ship lost in battle, a vessel wrecked by an iceberg, e even a surfer rescued by a family of dolphins are some of exciting tales of struggle and survival that will keep you on edge of your seat.

ISBN: 978-0-7760-3665-9

TRUE UNDERGROUND RESCUE STORIES

The harrowing tales of a baby trapped in a well, a man look for caves in Kentucky, coal miners and gold miners put deadly predicaments, and a man rescuing another from oncoming subway train.

ISBN: 978-0-7660-3676-5

TRUE WILDERNESS RESCUE STORIES

Read about thrilling rescues that took place in the wild, suc how a person was saved from a burning forest fire, and ho group of friends was rescued by their dog.

ISBN: 978-0-7660-3666-6